7-DAY LI

CW00419269

LEARN LENORMAND CARD READING IN A WEEK

Andrea Green

Forge Press: Keswick 2018.

Website: www.mytarotcardmeanings.com

Email: pa@celestialcanopy.com

About the Author

Andrea Green is the pen-name of a fortune-telling insider. Her first book, *True Tarot Card Meanings* went straight to #1 in Tarot books worldwide (Kindle and Print) where it has remained as the top-selling book for Tarot for over a year!

She has spent many years reading and researching cartomancy, divination and the esoteric arts. Her life is dedicated to sharing the knowledge that she has accumulated over the years. She believes that there should be no mystery in divination and is dedicated to helping every person discover fortune-telling for themselves.

If you are interested in further Lenormand courses, check out the classes for every level at:

www.tarotassociation.net

Learn Lenormand in Seven Days

Author Andrea Green boils down her extensive experience with the original Lenormand deck and presents these essential seven steps for you to learn Lenormand in just one week.

Andrea has worked with author Tali Goodwin who gave her exclusive access to the research that brought about the revival in Lenormand card reading. Now you can share – for the first time – the true interpretations and all the card meanings in one place!

This easy-to-follow booklet combines the earliest sources of fortune-telling by cards with the latest methods of teaching. It will give you the easiest and fastest way to read Lenormand cards with confidence.

As an experienced reader, you can also use this book as an essential reference guide to historical and contemporary card meanings.

You are about to learn Lenormand from the first roots of the tradition to the latest branches!

CONTENTS

Preface

The Lenormand Deck is a set of 36 cards with easy-to-read symbols such as the Dog and the Tree, the Lady and the Child. The cards have simple meanings such as 'friend' or 'health', 'a wife', or 'younger person'. It is a very literal deck and ideal for fortune-telling, resolving everyday situations and getting quick answers. In fact, it can also be used for deeper spiritual questions and provide a lot of detail in just a few cards.

The deck is read in a different way to tarot or oracle decks, in a particular language – which is very easy to learn. In this book you will be given the essential steps to learn Lenormand in just seven days and set off on a life-time journey of discovery with the cards.

You will also learn the actual history of the cards, which are nothing to do with the famous fortune-teller of Paris, Mlle. Lenormand, whose name is associated with the deck. The cards now known as Lenormand were actually designed in Germany as a game by the owner of a brass factory.

In this book are several learning methods that are **absolutely unique** - you'll not find these anywhere else!

Introduction

The Dog is in the House.

What can we say about this?

It is a friendly dog. The house is safe and comfortable.

The dog has been there a long time.

It protects the home and is loved by the family.

The house has been there a long time.

It has held many families and lives, over many years.

If that were a dream, or a story, it would be a nice one.

If that were a dream in answer to a question, it would be an answer that would say "you are safe with a loyal friend".

And the Lenormand cards are as simple as that. They are pictures of dreams which can answer your questions.

No matter the question. If you had asked, "Will my new job be OK?", "Is this a good car to purchase", or "Is Kim going to be trustworthy?" you would get your answer.

Two cards – the Dog and the House. Now let's meet the others.

Choosing Your Deck

There have been more Lenormand decks produced in the last six years than in the last two centuries, such is the new interest in this deck.

The original Lenormand deck is the best deck to buy, as it is a reproduction of the *Game of Hope* on which every Lenormand deck is based. It can be purchased from www.thegamecrafter.com.

You can also pick up a Blue Owl deck, which is one of the older decks.

If you locate and browse the Learning Lenormand Facebook Group for Lenormand decks or look at the many decks produced with Kickstarter funding, you will find many from which to choose.

However, here is a quick checklist to help your decision – as well as finding one where you actually like the artwork:

1. Can you tell the Clouds from the Ship or Star? The Ways from the Mountain or the Garden? It is important to easily be able to tell the cards from one another as soon as you look at them.

2. Is each card just simple symbols or full of symbols? Some new decks can be confusing because, for example, they might picture the Ways at the bottom of a mountain, or a Dog with a large sun in the design. It then becomes harder to tell which card you are looking at, if it has other symbols on it. The cards ideally should show just one symbol.

3. Can the deck be easily shuffled and laid out in a Grand Tableaux? If you want to master the largest spread, it requires space to lay out all 36 cards. Is the deck a good size for this?

4. Do the cards clearly show numbers and playing card inserts? When you discover later counting methods or correspondences with the playing cards, these will be useful. You do not necessarily need them as a beginner.

5. Does the designer understand the sources of the symbols and has referenced them correctly? If you have a deck with a ferocious dog or a cartoon laughing whip, this is likely so far deviated from the original Lenormand that it should instead be considered a semi-related Oracle deck.

There is such a wide range of Lenormand decks out there, with more decks being created every month, so you will be sure to find the decks that work best for you!

All the links to many more resources can be found at the back of this book.

Day 1. THE GAME OF HOPE

Today, on our first day of a week of study, we look at the history of the Cards and begin to learn why it is essential – and easier - to know this history before we actually read the deck.

We will then look at some important exercises for practice today – taking a little time, all within just one day – ready for day two, where we really get reading.

In history, we start in Nuremberg, Germany, around 1799, with the production of a new parlour game, *The Game of Hope*, by J. K. Hechtel, a brass factory owner.

The game was played by laying out 36 cards in number sequence and then racing other players using dice, in a manner similar to "snakes and ladders". In fact, all such games derive from the earliest known format *A Game of Goose* and perhaps trace their ancestry even earlier back to the *Senet* game of ancient Egypt.

J. K. Hechtel (1799).

The *Game of Hope* was typical of such games and used on each card a simple symbol which was instantly recognizable to the European Christian of the time; a dog for faithfulness, a garden park for socializing, a Cross for suffering and an Anchor for hope or faith.

It also used symbols from popular fables which would be told around the typical European dining table or at bedtime; the cunning Fox, for example, appears from the *Reynard* stories. In another card from the *Game of Hope*, we see the Stork – this is illustrated as eating a Frog, which comes from a fable which tells the tale of what happens to frogs who get too big for their pond!

In the game, when a player landed on a particular card, an instruction was given in a little accompanying booklet, telling them whether they should pay a forfeit or receive rewards from another player, move forwards or drop backwards, etc. In some cases, the player would have to wait on a card until they threw a particular dice number, or another player landed on their position.

Why is it important to know this history?

Well, for example, when the *Game of Hope* was first used as a parlour game, that tale of Reynard the Fox would have been common knowledge. The Fox in the deck would have instantly been seen in this light; as the trickster and master manipulator, looking after number one. The whole European family would know this was the 'meaning' of the fox – it would not be seen any other way.

Here is an image of Reynard the Fox at the Ways. Interestingly, "The Ways" is another Lenormand card!

Reynard The Fox.

We can also see early meanings in the original instructions for the game. In the booklet, we see that the "cunning fox leads the player astray", actually taking them back to "the woods" symbolized by the Tree card! So, it is a somewhat tricky card when appearing in a fortune-telling reading, for both good and ill, depending on its context.

We could also look at the Bear card, for example, in career readings, in this historical context. The Bear appears in the cards as a powerful boss, employer (company), or already established power – sometimes as a mother.

The relationship between the Fox and the Bear, for me, comes from the original tales of Reynard, where the Bear features as an active character.

The Fox and the Bear in the tales of Reynard are recognised as self-interest versus the establishment. Reynard tricks the bear in a number of different ways, always taking advantage of the bear's self-confidence and single-mindedness. The Fox works by indirect methods, manipulation and controlling the communications between the various parties, to his own ends. The Fox (unlike the Snake in the grass – another Lenormand card) is an enemy in plain sight – just in that they look after number one.

We can have some sympathy for the fox though, as he (or she) is also employing his self-interest to look after and feed his family back at the den. In some Lenormand decks we see him stalking the chickens who are totally unaware of their role in the natural pecking order.

So, when someone asks me about career (or any other subject) in a reading, I always think of the context in which players would have played the original *Game of Hope*, and the stories they would have told each other from those images. These would have been informed by their own experience of the tales of the time, including Reynard the Fox.

And as a general rule, when looking at career questions in the biggest reading – which we will learn later this week – the Grand Tableau, I always consider where the Fox and the Bear are positioned relative to each other, and the cards between them.

Is the Fox able to overcome the Bear to secure his own position? Is the Bear bringing a Cross and Coffin to stop the Fox in his ways? How can the Fox get around the Bear, if the Bear is in the way of the Fishes ...? Considering these two cards as the querent and the established power in their career, and likening them to the tales of Reynard, really helps me make sense of a reading.

When weaving a tale of the Fox and Bear, we can see archetypal stories and characteristics of those animals written into (and out of) us. They play out in real life as self-interest versus establishment, and this immediately applies to the career aspects of a reading.

So, what has the *Game of Hope* got to do with Lenormand cards? Shortly after the death of the famous Parisian fortune-teller Mlle. Lenormand, which was fifty years after the death of J. K. Hechtel, an enterprising publisher decided to capitalise on the Hechtel's deck and Lenormand's name. They produced a deck of cards – a recreation of the Game of Hope and simply called it the "Little Game of Lenormand", suggesting that these were in fact the very cards that had been used by Mlle. Lenormand.

We know that it is unlikely that she even knew about this particular deck of cards, instead she probably used a 'Piquet' deck or 'Etteilla' fortune-telling deck for her readings.

So, the Lenormand cards are not Lenormand cards at all – they are the *Game of Hope*.

The original sources of the modern Lenormand cards are an important part of its heritage and help us easily to understand the way in which the card meanings can be interpreted in a modern reading.

Having covered that bit of history, we will now present todays exercises to get us warmed up for the week. I suggest performing the exercises as close to given as possible, as many times during a day that is convenient for you. They are designed to build up together, so try and avoid the temptation to skip 'easy' exercises in favour of the more involved ones.

Each individual exercise has a particular and important skill to teach, which will get you set up for reading the Grand Tableaux by the end of the week. The exercises are also designed to get you to a confident position in a week from which you can then develop further skills.

If you are already a confident reader, this book can be used as a reference guide to the essential meanings of each card and other useful reading skills.

EXERCISE 1

Take your deck and ensure that the cards are arranged by number. Look through the cards, counting them out aloud, saying both with the name of the card and the number. It is very important for later this week that you say both the name and the number.

EXERCISE 2

Lay all the cards out in your deck in **four** rows of **nine** cards. Say each card out aloud whilst looking through them in order, like this "The Rider THEN the Clover THEN the Ship ..."

Notice particularly the cards at the start and end of each row, in the corners, the cards in the middle, etc. Get used to scanning around the layout to get familiar with the designs, the images, and their locations.

Treat this exercise a little bit like a memory game.

Repeat these two simple exercises as many times as possible during the day. There is no test, other than to get familiar with the deck and an idea of the positions when laid out in a four by nine pattern.

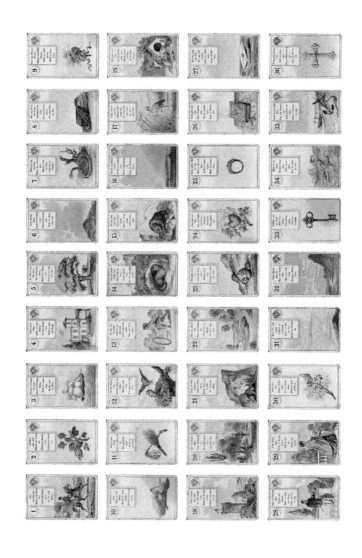

All 36 cards in order.

Day 2. A JOCULAR GAME

Today we discover the *Coffee Cards*, adding to our historical knowledge, and learn to start reading the Lenormand cards.

The *Game of Hope* was not the first deck of cards to use the symbols we now see – although as we saw yesterday it did become the model of the Lenormand deck. There was an earlier deck called the Coffee Cards, produced in a book, *The Games of Germany* (1796), a copy of which presently sits in the British Museum.

The Coffee Cards in that book are very similar to the Lenormand deck with a few variants. We do not need to look at these differences in this 7-day sprint, just to know one particular thing, which is really important.[1]

In the Coffee Cards book, it is clearly stated – for the first time in print – that **the card symbols are based on the divinatory reading of coffee grounds**.

So, when you are doing a Lenormand reading, you are actually doing a picture-book version of coffee grounds or tea-leaf reading! Which are both based in turn on the most ancient form of divination – dream symbolism.

Perhaps this is why Lenormand cards are so simple and direct – they are a defined set of symbols taken from our most basic experience of dreams, where there is an overlap between the outer and inner worlds.

A JOCULAR TALE

So, we learnt yesterday that the Lenormand cards are a reprint of the earlier *Game of Hope* cards. This was a Christian teaching game – likely only on the basis that it would allow for the cards to be also used for gambling!

The second important thing for our rapid race through the deck is that the original *Game of Hope* booklet also gave a simple instruction (in German) for fortune-telling by the cards:

"With these same cards it is also possible to play an entertaining game of oracles by shuffling the 36 cards and then letting the person, for whom the oracle is meant, cut the cards, then laying out the cards in 5 rows with 4 rows at 8 cards each and the 5th row with the remaining 4 cards. If the person querying is a woman, one starts from card 29, spinning a jocular tale from the cards nearby around the figures on display. If it is for a man, the tale is started from card 28 and again makes use of the cards surrounding this one. This will bring much entertainment to any merry company".[2]

And that was it – the instructions were simply to compose a "jocular tale". There is almost an instruction in there that the oracle is for entertainment purposes only. Perhaps that line as used nowadays traces itself back all the way to an old hang-up about the cards being used in a non-Christian way rather than a modern legal requirement!

So, today, having looked over the cards yesterday, let's look at several pairs of cards. We try not to learn Lenormand by one card at a time - they really do read far better and easier with more than one card.

If we remember our introduction at the start of this book, we know that we can make a simple tale about a Dog and a House.

What about a Snake and a Child?

That gives a far more ominous title to a story! The child will not know there is danger, and the snake may have a nasty bite.

Now that we know that we can make intuitive stories from pictures, we add a little bit of language magick to our 'saying out loud' exercises. This makes a small – but important – step into reading the cards.

We will not stick with this purely 'intuitive' approach, as the cards have specific meanings, but it is a fine place to start and a useful skill to develop.

The Snake and the Child.

Exercise 1

Here are some titles for stories.

Imagine the first few lines or think about what *sort* of story they would be and what might be happening in it:

The Gentleman and the Fox

The Dog and the Child

The Bear in the Tower

The Key of the Moon

The Bouquet at the Crossroads

Take your time and think about each one several times before deciding on your response. There is no 'correct answer' for these - just allow your natural response to be a guide.

Exercise 2

Now that you have considered five tales, select out **two cards** from your deck and create a tale yourself – or simply write down the title and think about what sort of story it would be.

You are now already on your way to learning Lenormand by reading it as it was instructed in the original game!

Optional Exercise

Try reading **three** cards by putting them in the following sentence structure:

[CARD 1] BECAUSE OF

[CARD 2] BECAUSE OF

[CARD 3]

So, if we had MOUNTAIN + HEART + GARDEN, this would read:

MOUNTAIN BECAUSE OF

HEART BECAUSE OF

GARDEN.

We have a Mountain, which seems like a serious obstacle or difficult challenge, knowing what we know of mountains, because of Heart – a romance, perhaps – because of a Garden? That makes us think about a Shakespeare play where everyone meets in a garden, but there is confusion. So, someone met someone, fell in love, but it has led to a current obstacle ... this easily sounds like a Lenormand reading.

You try it!

You will notice we have not even covered the 'meaning' of the cards yet – we will do this tomorrow, trusting that we can all respond to the natural symbolism used in the deck, unlike the obscure and esoteric symbolism sometimes used in tarot decks.

Day 3. LENORMAND CARDS

Today we meet all the cards and start to quickly widen our experience in reading cards from the whole deck.

A lot of so-called 'traditions' or 'schools' or 'styles' of Lenormand reading have been suggested, but only by people within the last few years. Different decks, books, languages, locations and authors have all modified the meanings of the cards, extended them, and copied them over time from the original sources.

The original 'meanings' of the cards generally came from a sheet which was issued with the earliest 'Lenormand' cards and was said to have been written by "Philippe LeNormand". This person did not exist and was used as a marketing ploy.

As we know, the cards themselves published as 'Lenormand' were not those used by Mlle. Lenormand.

In the following section, I have provided a reference page for each card and given a set of meanings starting with the 'Phillipe Sheet' (c. 1846) in *italics* and working historically through the earliest dream symbolism, prior meanings given in the *Coffee Cards* (1796) and *Game of Hope* instructions (1799), followed by later meanings from A. E. Waite (1909, writing on coffee grounds) and finally offering several contemporary meanings.

I have also provided my own 'functional' interpretation of each card as it might be used in a general sense, where the specific meaning may not immediately fit a precise situation. Sometimes the MICE may mean 'little bits' rather than an actual thief, which would be nonsense for every time it appeared in a reading.

If you wish to read the cards in a historical manner, you can simply use the first set of meanings in each case, or if you prefer to use contemporary meanings, you can ignore any contradictory historical sets of meanings.

The historical meanings also include game instructions which we can ignore in this context other than that they might indicate if the card was a positive or negative card such as "lose 4 marks" being negative or "advance 6 cards" being positive.

Some cards may not have the same amount of references as others because the *Game of Hope* and *Coffee Cards* differed by several card images and the game does not have a specific rule for every card.

If you would like to use the cards for universal themes, or for deeper, psychological and spiritual readings, consult the dream symbolism section for each card. I have taken these from a variety of symbolism books, including Cirlot. They provide a universal language suited in extending the cards to more profound and powerful readings.

At the end of each card section, I have then written a "what you say" sentence for basic practice and when reading for yourself, to ensure the cards speak directly and simply.[3]

Before I introduce all the cards, here is the exercise for today which will quickly get you familiar with reading the deck.

Exercise 1

Think of a small question to ask the cards, even if it is "Tell me what is important for me to know". Shuffle the deck and lay out **three** cards from left to right. Now consult the cards in the following section and join together the "what you say" quotes for the cards (which you will find under each card description) with any combination of these linking words:

And ... so ... when ... as ... because ... if ... but ...

That is to say, if you drew FISH + HOUSE + DOG you might combine the quotes like so:

The Fish bring resources **and** the House is secure **because** the Dog is a friend.

You can simply use "and" as the connecting word if this is easiest for you – just find what works best for you.

Depending on the question, this reading would indicate that we can benefit in our security through a friend, rather than trying to do something about it by ourselves.

If you feel like using more meaningful linking words or extending the sentence even further, elaborating more on a particular card, then do so – as long as you try and stick to the meanings here and do not wander too far away.

Fish + House + Dog

Try different draws of cards and different questions today for your practice and to get used to reading the card meanings in different ways.

You might like to journal your exercises at this point or repeat the earlier exercises for further practice until you are comfortable. There is no need to rush to get everything done in seven days – take whatever time you require.

THE CARDS

1. The Rider (Cavalier)

is a messenger of good fortune – if not surrounded by unlucky cards, brings good news, which the Person may expect, either from his own house or from abroad; this will, however, not take place immediately, but some time later.

Dream Symbolism: In myth and folklore a horse was portrayed as a clairvoyant animal. The horse corresponds to Mars and people believed that the sudden appearance of a horse portended news of war and disruption. Clairvoyance. Dreams. Bad News. A Herald.

Coffee Cards: DENOTES good news from abroad, in money matters, a good situation in a foreign, or good prospects. He that doubts his fortune, is promised a lasting one by this emblem.

Coffee Card Verse: Despair not of Men's goodness for you shall have an unexpected proof of it; you may expect news, and restitution of that which you thought lost.

Game of Hope: N/A

Waite: Someone who will fight (espouse) your cause.

Contemporary: News, new information. Innovation, surprise.

Functional: Novelty.

What You Say: The Rider brings news.

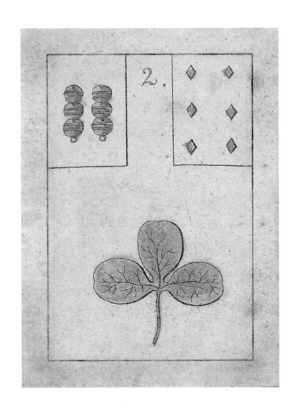

2. The Clover Leaf

is also a harbinger of good news; but if surrounded by clouds it indicates great pain; but if No 2 [Clover] lies near No. 29 [Lady] or No. 28 [Gentleman], the pain will be of short duration, and soon change to a happy issue.

Dream Symbolism: The Trinity. Divine nature. Mountain clover was a sign of success through perseverance and faith; making your own luck. Perseverance. Divine Reward.

Coffee Cards: Is as well here as in common life a lucky sign.

Its different position in the cup alone makes the difference; because, if it is on the top, it shews that the good Fortune is not far distant, but it is subject to delay, if it is in the middle or at the bottom. Should clouds surround it, it shews that many disagreeables will attend the good Fortune; in the clear, it prognosticates serene and undisturbed happiness, as bright as the party wishes.

Coffee Card Verse: You may be very fortunate indeed if you always discharge your duty with honor and integrity.

Game of Hope: N/A

Waite: Speedy Good Fortune

Contemporary: A little bit of luck, small gains, a little success.

Functional: Minor positive change.

What You Say: The Clover brings a little luck.

3. The Ship

the symbol of commerce, signifies great wealth, which will be acquired by trade or inheritance; if near to the Person, it means an early journey.

Dream Symbolism: The journey, often into the unknown – or the unconscious. Transition and self-development. New shores. Gathering oneself together for a new phase of life.

Coffee Cards: N/A

Coffee Card Verse: N/A

Game of Hope: The one, who throws 3 pips and thus gets to the Ship, will be happily taken by this ship to the Canary Islands, where the well-known beautiful birds are at home, no. 12.

Waite: N/A

Contemporary: Travel, risk, adventure, speculation.

Functional: Movement.

What You Say: The Ship means risk.

4. The House

is a certain sign of success and prosperity in all undertakings; and although the present position of the Person may be disagreeable, yet the future will be bright and happy. If this card lies in the centre of the cards, under the Person, this is a hint to beware of those who surround him or her.

Dream Symbolism: Protection and security. The Self or Psyche. The house can also represent the human body, the exterior is the front we give out to the world, the interior contains our inner realm; our mind, emotions and the soul that it shelters.

Coffee Cards: INDICATES, at the top of the cup, blessing and success in all your enterprises; if your situation be then not the most favourable, you may hope that it soon will change for the better. In the middle, or below, it cautions you to be vigilant over your servants, as your vigilance alone will prevent you being injured.

Coffee Card Verse: From the visit which you and your house will receive, great advantages must ensue, but let prudence guide your conduct.

Game of Hope: On entry in this House, two marks have to be given up to the doorkeeper.

Waite: House.

Contemporary: Home, family, security.

Functional: Stability.

What You Say: The House is security.

5

Ein Baum thut
Dir kund,
Du bleibst stets
gesund,
Sind's der Bäume
viel,
Kommst Du bald
an's Ziel.

Another Version of the Tree card with German Verse.

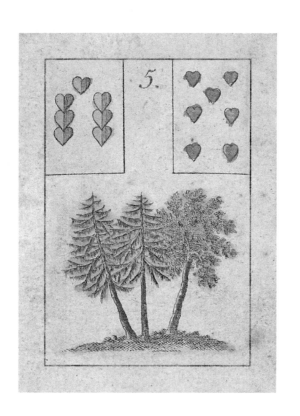

5. A Tree

if distant from the Person, signifies good health; more trees of different cards together leave no doubt about the realization of all reasonable wishes.

Dream Symbolism: Symbolic of the strong life-force, durability and even immortality. The tree connects the earth and the heavens as it has its roots in the earth and its branches touch the sky. Spiritual wellbeing and holistic healing. Connection to the highest principles and our deepest sources.

Coffee Cards: One tree only, be it in clear, or thick part, points out lasting good health; several trees denote that your wish will be accomplished. If they are encompassed with dashes, it is a token that your fortune is in blossom. And will require some time to bring it to maturity. If they are accompanied by dots, it is a sign that you will make your fortune in the country where you reside.

Coffee Card Verse: Never regret labor or pains; a good work is its own reward, be this your consolation. The industrious, in whose number you are comprised, will never want for lucre and decent support.

Game of Hope: N/A

Waite: Health.

Contemporary: Health. Longevity, strong roots.

Functional: Support.

What You Say: The Tree is health.

The Tree and Clouds, an uncertainty with health.

Another Version of the Tree with Playing Card Insert.

6. Clouds

if their clear side is turned towards the Person, are a lucky sign; with the dark side turned to the Person, something disagreeable will soon happen.

Dream Symbolism: Changeability. Portent, Signs, a Celestial Messenger. Accepting unstable conditions.

Coffee Cards: If they be more light than dark, you may expect a good result from your hopes, but if they are black, you may give it up. Surrounded with dots they imply success in trade, and in all your undertakings, but the brighter they are, the greater will be your happiness.

Coffee Card Verse: Just as the clouds are dispelled, so let your anger vanish, then you will soon be superior to all vexations.

Game of Hope: The Thundercloud drives back to no. 2

Waite: Happiness (Misfortune)

Contemporary: Confusion, uncertainty, change, loss of direction.

Functional: Misdirection.

What You Say: The Clouds brings uncertainty.

7. Snake (Serpent)

is a sign of misfortune, the extent of which depends upon the greater or smaller distance from the Person; it is followed invariably by deceit, infidelity and sorrow.

Dream Symbolism: Potential for Energy or Evil. Mutability. But also, temptation, something that will lead you astray from your path. The snake has regenerative capabilities, so on a positive note, resurrection and renewal. Kundalini, harnessing sexual energy.

Coffee Cards: ALWAYS the emblem of falsehood and enmity. On the top or in the middle of the cup, it promises to the consulting party the triumph which he desires over his enemy. But he will not obtain it so easily, if the serpent be in the thick or cloudy part. By the letter which frequently appears near the emblem, the enemy may easily be guessed, it makes the initial of his name.

Coffee Card Verse: A secret enemy endeavours to injure you; try by kindness to make him your friend.

Game of Hope: To stay safe from the bite of this dangerous Snake, 3 marks have to be paid.

Waite: Treachery, an Enemy.

Contemporary: Betrayal, deception, deceit, lies, distrust, danger.

Functional: Attack.

What You Say: The Snake is betrayal.

Here the Snake is in the Man's past, likely through a recent
work-related issue (Fox).

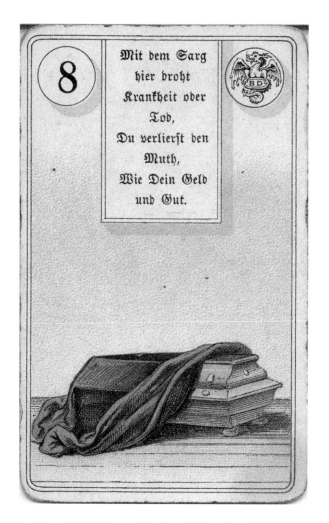

Another Version of the Coffin with German Verse.

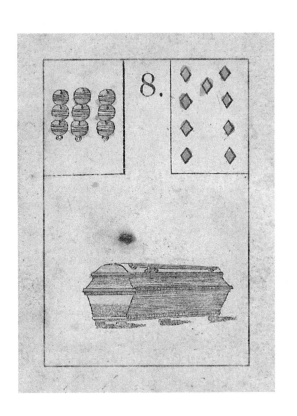

8. A Coffin

very near to the Person, means, without any doubt, dangerous diseases, death or a total loss of fortune. More distant from the Person, the card is less dangerous.

Dream Symbolism: End of an attachment to the material life and embarking on a more spiritual life. Initiation.

Coffee Cards: The emblem of death prognosticates the same thing here, or at least a long and tedious illness, if it be in the thick or turbid. In the clear, it denotes long life. In the thick at the tip of the cup, it signifies a considerable estate left to the party by some rich relation; in the same manner at the bottom, it shews that the deceased is not so nearly related to the consulting party.

Coffee Card Verse: You may rejoice at a considerable legacy, but many people will envy you for it.

Game of Hope: The one who gets to this Coffin is deemed to be dead until another player comes to this sheet or until he casts a double, for when it his turn to roll the dice he is not excluded.

Waite: N/A

Contemporary: End, Stop, completion.

Functional: Finality.

What You Say: The Coffin brings an end.

9. The Bouquet (Flowers)

means much happiness in every respect.

Dream Symbolism: Gift of language. Diplomacy. The appreciation of others. Empathy. Sympathy. Presenting oneself in a complete way.

Coffee Cards: The greatest success in any science or art; if the consulting party be married, he may expect good children, and all the fruits to be expected from their good education in his old age.

Coffee Card Verse: You sport with fortune, but whatever the cards refuse, your good sense, your skill, and learning will amply compensate.

Game of Hope: N/A

Waite: Joy, Happiness, Peaceful Life. The most fortunate of Omens.

Contemporary: Gift, appreciation, bonus.

Functional: Presentation, a Showing.

What You Say: The Bouquet brings a gift.

10. The Scythe

indicates great danger, which will only be avoided if lucky cards surround it.

Dream Symbolism: Death but also rebirth – a timely death of what must be harvested. A point in a natural cycle. If the scythe is curved, a lunar symbol of regular change. If a long scythe, a symbol of Saturn and a deeper transformation.

Coffee Cards: If combined with an hour-glass, it denotes imminent dangers of all kinds. Below, it signifies a long and happy life.

Coffee Card Verse: Wait quietly for the harvest, proportionate to your labor; for every one is the maker of his own fortune.

Game of Hope: N/A

Waite: N/A

Contemporary: Cutting, clearing, doing away with, harvesting.

Functional: Time.

What You Say: The Scythe means cutting.

11. The Rod (Birch)

means quarrels in the family, domestic afflictions, want of peace amongst married persons; also fever and protracted sickness.

Dream Symbolism: Punishment. The whip used to overwhelm and overpower another. Domination. Abuse of power or imbalanced power relationship. Inner struggle. Guilt. Shame.

Coffee Cards: SHEWS differences with relations about matters relating to legacies; in the thick, illness.

Coffee Card Verse: You are involved in disputes. Do not engage in them too warmly else your body will be afflicted with illness.

Game of Hope: So as not to be castigated by this Rod, one pays two marks. For this one can move forward two more sheets – to the Lad on No. 13.

Waite: N/A

Contemporary: Strife, conflict, argument, ill feeling, punishment, retribution.

Functional: Control.

What You Say: The Whip is strife.

12. Birds (A Bird)

means hardships to overcome, but of short duration; distant from the Person, it means the accomplishment of a pleasant journey.

Dream Symbolism: The human soul. Messenger of the Divine. Higher thoughts and communication. A call for clarity in the crowd, whether within or without.

Coffee Cards: In the clear it signifies, that the disagreeables and troubles, with which you shall have to combat, will soon be over; in the thick, it is a sign of good living, and of a speedy successful journey or voyage, which, if there are dashes will be directed to a great distance.

Coffee Card Verse: You are very happy, but love entirely swayed by passion will render you very unhappy.

Game of Hope: N/A

Waite: Good Omen, Sudden Stroke of Luck.

Contemporary: Gossip, chatter, social media, distraction.

Functional: Two, Pair.

What You Say: Birds reveal distractions and chatter.

13. The Child

is a sign that the Person moves in good society and is full of kindness towards everybody.

Dream Symbolism: The child is seen as symbolising an investment in the future. A youthful energy, something that will start anew. A connection to a more soulful way of being. Living in a simplistic manner. Return to innocence. The Inner Child.

Coffee Cards: In the clear part it bespeaks innocent intercourse between the consulter and person, in the thick part, excesses in love matters, attended with great expense; at the bottom of the cup, it denotes the consequences of libidinous amours.

Coffee Card Verse: The consequences of the good education which you will give to your children, shall gladden your old age. You shall live to see much joy from them.

Game of Hope: N/A

Waite:

Contemporary: Innocence, immaturity.

Functional: Undeveloped.

What You Say: The Child is young.

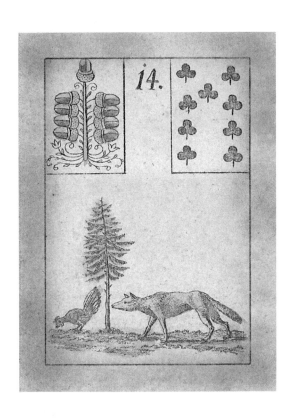

14. The Fox

if near, is a sign to mistrust persons with whom you are connected, because some of them try to deceive you; if distant, no danger is to be apprehended.

Dream Symbolism: In the middle ages the Fox was often used to represent the devil. This suggests a devious character, a trickster, a fraud. Living inauthentically. A manipulator or manipulation.

Coffee Cards: N/A

Coffee Card Verse: N/A

Game of Hope: The cunning Fox leads the player astray and he has to find refuge in the Wood at no. 5.

Waite: Trouble and Difficulties.

Contemporary: Cunning, sly, work, self-sufficiency, devious, manipulator.

Functional: Self.

What You Say: The Fox is cunning.

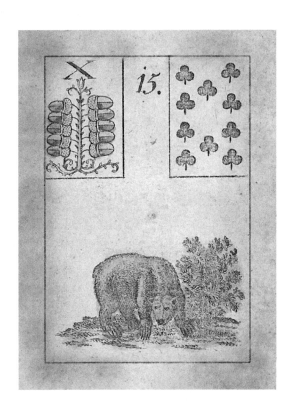

15. The Bear

is either a messenger of good fortune, or admonishes us to keep away from company; particularly that of the envious.

Dream Symbolism: In the alchemical process the bear corresponds to the *nigredo* of *prima materia*, the death phase of the first matter. It symbolises an influence from our baser instincts. The Shadow. A 'dark night of our soul'. Overwhelming fear.

Coffee Cards: AT the top in the clear, it signifies all kind of prosperity with people of quality. At the bottom it warns the consulter to shun all such intercourse, as he will at all events find persons who will envy him his fortune, and not see it with indifference.

Coffee Card Verse: Be always on your guard; he easily believes is easily deceived.

Game of Hope: N/A

Waite: Trouble and Difficulties.

Contemporary: Authority, mother, headstrong, power.

Functional: Force.

What You Say: The Bear means a strong person.

16. The Star

confirms good luck in all enterprises; but if near clouds, it means a long series of unhappy accidents.

Dream Symbolism: The Spirit. The Will. Life Spark. A light in the dark. Hope. A symbol of destiny. Chance of divine navigation through signs and symbols. Head to a brighter future.

Coffee Cards: Denotes happiness if in the clear, and at the top of the cup; clouded or in the thick it signifies long life, though exposed to various troubles. If dots are about it, it foretells great fortune, wealth, high respectability, & c. Several stars denote so many good and happy children, but surrounded with dashes, shews that your children will cause you grief vexation in your old age, and that you ought to prevent it by giving them a good education in time.

Coffee Card Verse: Do your part, and you will soon experience the good effects of it.

Game of Hope: Arriving at the Star of good prospects, the player receives 6 marks.

Waite: Happiness, Success.

Contemporary: Direction, navigation, luck.

Functional: Vision.

What You Say: The Star reveals direction.

17. The Stork

indicates a change of abode which will take place, the sooner the nearer the card lies to the Person.

Dream Symbolism: Family. Duty. The stork can be relied upon to return home and look after its affairs. Tradition. Examining behaviour in the light of parents and upbringing. Becoming a Wayfarer. Recognising lineage. Understanding parental roles. Perhaps the need for a ritual.

Coffee Cards: N/A

Coffee Card Verse: N/A

Game of Hope: N/A

Waite: N/A

Contemporary: Delivery, return, birth.

Functional: Habit.

What You Say: The Stork brings a return.

18. The Dog

if near the Person, you can consider your friends faithful and sincere; but if very distant and surrounded by clouds, be cautious not to trust those who call themselves your friends.

Dream Symbolism: As generally, a symbol of faithfulness. Also, a Companion. Psychic Protection. The need to show teeth in some way. Take yourself from a leash. Make Territory within or without.

Coffee Cards: BEING at all times the emblem of fidelity or envy, has also a two-fold meaning here. At the top, in the clear, it signifies true and faithful friends, but if his image be surrounded with clouds and dashes, it shews that those whom you take for your friends are not to be depended upon; but if the dog be at the bottom of the cup, you have to dread the effects of extreme envy or jealousy.

Coffee Card Verse: You will easily find better friends among strangers than among your own relations.

Game of Hope: N/A

Waite: A Friend.

Contemporary: Faithful Friend, close companion, trust.

Functional: Closeness.

What You Say: The Dog is a friend.

19. The Tower

gives the hope of a happy old age; but if surrounded by clouds, it forebodes sickness, and, according to circumstances, even death.

Dream Symbolism: The influence of a higher power. The Tower is a symbol of ascent. Attainment of a spiritual realm or state of being. Transcendence from the material to the spiritual. The building of a life from earth to heaven. Advantage.

Coffee Cards: N/A

Coffee Card Verse: N/A

Game of Hope: To enjoy the pleasant vista from the Tower, one pays 2 marks.

Waite: N/A

Contemporary: Bureaucracy, institutions, government, authority, border, separation, law.

Functional: Observation.

What You Say: The Tower is an institution.

20. Garden (The Park)

prognosticates that you will visit a very respectable company; if very near, that you are to form a very intimate friendship, but if distant, it hints of false friends.

Dream Symbolism: The civilisation of nature; a place where nature has been tamed. Sanctuary. A time to withdraw. Cultivate. Meditation. A meeting of oneself. Time to appreciate.

Coffee Cards: SIGNIFIES a large company. In the clear, it indicates good friends, of which it will consist; in the thick, or encompassed with streaks, it warns the consulting party to be cautious, and not to take for his friends those who merely profess themselves as such.

Coffee Card Verse: You frequently go into company, if you wish to be benefited by it, hear much and say little.

Game of Hope: N/A

Waite: N/A

Contemporary: Networking, socialising, parties, conferences, meetings, society.

Functional: Connection.

What You Say: The Garden is a meeting place.

21. Mountain (The Mountains)

near the Person, warn you against a mighty enemy; if distant, you may rely on powerful friends.

Dream Symbolism: Symbolic of spiritual elevation and overcoming obstacles. The work of endurance in the journey. Preparing for a long game.

Coffee Cards: If it represent only one mountain, it indicates the favour of people of high rank, but several of them, especially in the thick, are signs of powerful enemies, in the clear, they signify the contrary, or friends in high life, who are endeavouring to promote the consulting.

Coffee Card Verse: You may easily get in favour with the great, but remember always that the higher you rise the deeper you will fall.

Game of Hope: On these steep Alps, the player has to remain until another arrives to release him or he has to cast a double.

Waite: Friends (Enemies)

Contemporary: Obstacle, diversion.

Functional: Effort.

What You Say: The Mountain is an obstruction.

22. The Ways (Roads, Crossroads)

surrounded by clouds, are signs of disaster; but without this card, and if distant from [the] Person, that you shall find ways and means to avoid the threatening danger.

Dream Symbolism: Symbolic of the union of opposites. Reconciliation. A new path. Opportunity to make a change of direction. Very dependent on other cards in this regard.

Coffee Cards: Or serpentine lines indicate ways; if they are covered with clouds, and consequently in the thick, they are said to be infallible marks, either of many past or future reverses. But, if they appear in the clear and serene, they are the surest token of some fortunate chance near at hand, encompassed with many points or dots they signify an accidental gain of money, likewise long life.

Coffee Card Verse: Excesses will certainly make you unhappy, avoid them therefore while it is time.

Game of Hope: Unnoticed, this path leads around the mountains right back to the Garden at no. 20.

Waite: N/A

Contemporary: Choice, decision, crossroads.

Functional: Options.

What You Say: The Ways mean a choice.

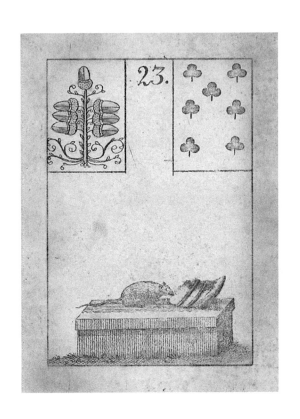

23. Mice (The Mouse)

is a sign of theft, a loss; when near, it indicates the recovery of the thing lost or stolen; if at a distance, the loss will be irreparable.

Dream Symbolism: A mouse in medieval symbolism was associated with the devil. The mouse is known to nibble away at material possessions, in the very same way that the devil would be constantly nibbling away at the resolve of man to stay on the right path. Spiritually then, not giving into our inferior nature, the small but destructive voice within ourselves.

Coffee Cards: As this animal lives by stealth, it is also an emblem here of theft or robbery; it is also an emblem here of theft or robbery; if it be in the clear, it shews that you will get again what you lost in a wonderful manner, but if it appears in the thick you may renounce this hope.

Coffee Card Verse: Have a vigilant eye upon your servants, as your negligence may make an honest man a thief.

Game of Hope: N/A

Waite: Trouble and Difficulties.

Contemporary: Loss, theft, small bites.

Functional: Small, Little, By Incremental Steps.

What You Say: The Mice means little bites.

24. The Heart

is a sign of joy leading to union and bliss.

Dream Symbolism: Unity. The love of the divine. Love in its widest or deepest sense. Union. Our true inner centre. Compassion and care, either within or without – or both.

Coffee Cards: If it be in the clear, it signifies future pleasure. It promises joy at receiving some money, if surrounded with dots. If a ring, or two hearts be together, it signifies, that the party is about to be married or betrothed; if a letter be perceptible near it, it shows the initial of the person's name; if the letter be in the clear, the party is a virgin; if in the thick, a widow.

Coffee Card Verse: You meditate a project of marriage, if you consult reason, you will abound with blessings.

Game of Hope: Whoever wins this Heart, will immediately offer it to the Youth at no. 28 or to the Girl at no. 29. That is to say, if the player arriving at the card 24 is a woman, she will move up to 28, if it is a man to 29.

Waite: Joy.

Contemporary: Love, romance, relationship, union.

Functional: Contentment.

What You Say: The Heart is love.

25. The Ring

if on the right of the Person, prognosticates a rich and happy marriage; when on the left, and distant, a falling out with the object of your affection, and the breaking off of a marriage.

Dream Symbolism: Continuity. Eternity. A situation or pattern, feeling or behaviour, coming full cycle. Commitment to one's own centre. A negative cycle of behaviour. Potential for evolution.

Coffee Cards: SIGNIFIES marriages; if a letter is near it [footnote: This means only something similar to a letter, as it has already been observed respecting the figures in the cup in general], it denotes to the person that has his Fortune told, the initial of the name of the party to be married.

Coffee Card Verse: In the happy marriage which you are about to enter; avoid Jealousy for the sake of your own peace of mind.

Married. If the ring is in the clear, it portends happy and lucrative friendship. Surrounded with clouds, designs that the party is to use precaution in the friendship he is about to contract, least he should be insidiously deceived, but it is most inauspicious, it the ring appears at the bottom of the cup, as it forebodes an entire separation from the beloved object.

Game of Hope: Whoever finds this Ring, gets 3 marks.

Waite: Marriage

Contemporary: Contract, marriage, agreement, oath, commitment.

Functional: Binding.

What You Say: The Ring is commitment.

Another version of the Book with German Verse.

26. The Book

indicates that you are going to find out a secret; according to its position, you can judge in what manner; great caution, however, is necessary in attempting a solution.

Dream Symbolism: A creation. Making our own story. Examining a story being told. The narrative we tell ourselves. History – personal of family. Sometimes, the unknown pattern we keep hidden.

Coffee Cards: N/A

Coffee Card Verse: N/A

Game of Hope: Whoever reads in this Grimoire will by a hex therein be forcefully returned to the Garden in No. 20.

Waite: N/A

Contemporary: Secret, Knowledge, Learning.

Functional: A Lesson.

What You Say: The Book brings knowledge.

27. The Letter

without clouds, means luck, which comes to you by distant, favourable news; but if dark clouds are near the Person, you may expect much grief.

Dream Symbolism: Written communication. Things we tell ourselves or others. A need to connect.

Coffee Cards: By the letters we communicate to our friends either pleasant or unpleasant news, or such is the case here; if this emblem is in the clear part, it denotes the speedy arrival of welcome news;

Surrounded with dots, it announces the arrival of a considerable remittance in money; but hemmed in by clouds it is quite the contrary, and forebodes some melancholy or bad tidings, a loss, or some other sinister accident. If it be in the clear and accompanied by a heart, lovers may expect a letter, which secures to the party the possession of the beloved object. But in the thick it denotes a refusal.

Coffee Card Verse: You may flatter yourself with good hopes in your enterprise but act prudently and speak not always as you feel.

Game of Hope: Whoever receives this Letter has to pay a fee of 2 marks for the bearer.

Waite: News. Remittance. Bad Tidings. Journey.

Contemporary: Written Word, Record, text.

Functional: History (personal, learning from what has gone before, in other past situations).

What You Say: The Letter is writing and recording.

A Lenormand Card Reading in Progress (2012).

28. The Gentleman

The Whole of the pack refers to either of these cards, depending, if the person whose fortune is being told is either a Lady (No. 29) or Gentleman (No. 28).

Dream Symbolism: The masculine energies. The Animus.

Coffee Cards: DENOTES in general a merchant, good business, pleasant news, and recovery of lost things. It also signifies that the consulting party will soon enlist, or get some engagement.

Coffee Card Verse: Depend upon receiving some good news; the loss you have sustained will recover likewise.

Game of Hope: This Youth leads on to the brilliant Sun of hope in no. 31. However for those who got here by way of the Heart, No. 24, this does not happen. They wait here for the next turn.

Waite: Speedy Visitor.

Contemporary: Man, Analytical, masculine, force.

Functional: Paternal qualities.

What You Say: The Man is you or the other person in your life.

29. The Lady

The Whole of the pack refers to either of these cards, depending, if the person whose fortune is being told is either a Lady (No. 29) or Gentleman (No. 28).

Dream Symbolism: The feminine energies. The Anima.

Coffee Cards: Signifies much joy in general. If in the clear this emblem has a more favourable signification than in the thick; there it shews very great happiness; here a great deal of jealousy. If dots surround the image, it explains the lady's fertility, or her wealth. The different position in the cup, shews at the top and in the middle that you will be in love with a virgin, but at the bottom it marks that she is a widow.

Coffee Card Verse: Gratify your partiality to the fair sex, but never offend decency.

Game of Hope: The Girl leads on to no. 32, unless one has come here through the Heart.

Waite: N/A

Contemporary: Woman, Intuitive, feminine, form.

Functional: Maternal qualities.

What You Say: The Woman is you or the other person in your life.

30. The Lilies

indicate a happy life; surrounded by clouds, a family grief. If this card is placed above the Person, they indicate the same as being virtuous; if below the Person, the moral principles are doubted.

Dream Symbolism: As generally, an emblem of purity and virtue. The simple life of the soul. Pure Wisdom. Age. Memory, in some senses.

Coffee Cards: If this emblem be at the top, or in the middle of the cup, it signifies the consulting party either has, or will have a virtuous spouse, if it be at the bottom, it denotes quite the reverse. In the clear, the Lily further betokens long and happy life; if clouded, or in the thick, it portends trouble and vexation, especially on the part of one's relations.

Coffee Card Verse: You wish for a virtuous wife, this wish may be granted if you requite the same for the same.

Game of Hope: N/A

Waite: Happy Marriage (Anger)

Contemporary: Purity, Simplicity, alternatively Sex or Older Age.

Functional: Values.

What You Say: The Lily means purity.

31. The Sun

lying near, points to happiness and pleasure, as its beams spread light and warmth; far away, it indicates misfortune and sorrow, as without the Sun's influence nothing can grow.

Dream Symbolism: The Centre. The Self. The core of our being. Light.

Coffee Cards: An emblem of the greatest luck and happiness if in the clear; but in the thick, it bodes a great deal of sadness; surrounded by dots, or dashes, denotes that an alteration will easily take place.

Coffee Card Verse: You will make an unexpected fortune, use it so that no body may covet it.

Game of Hope: N/A

Waite: Happiness, Success.

Contemporary: A lot of luck, development, growth, Success.

Functional: Encouragement.

What You Say: The Sun is good luck.

32. The Moon

is a sign of great honors, fortune and fame, if the card lies at the side of the Person; if at a distance, it means grief and misery.

Dream Symbolism: The unconscious, dreams – particularly with the Rider (Horse) or Bear. Deep patterns. Tides. The feminine side of our nature – particularly with the Lady.

Coffee Cards: If it appears in the clear, it denotes high honours, in the dark or the thick part, it implies sadness, which will however pass without great prejudice. But if it be at the bottom of the cup, the consulting party will be very fortunate both by water and land.

Coffee Card Verse: The liberality of your mind will always rather increase than lessen your prosperity; it will also daily endear you more to your friends.

Game of Hope: N/A

Waite: Happiness, Success.

Contemporary: Fame, Recognition, Dreams, How others see you.

Functional: Reflection.

What You Say: The Moon brings recognition.

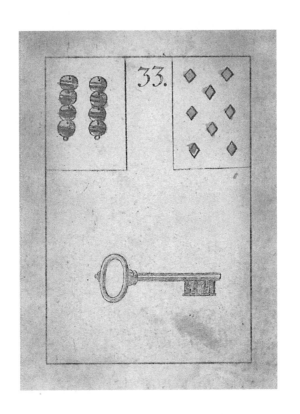

33. The Key

if near, means the certain success of a wish or a plan; if distant, the contrary.

Dream Symbolism: Revelation. Unlocking a pattern. Closing the door on something old or empty. Opening a new door through choice and action.

Coffee Cards: N/A

Coffee Card Verse: N/A

Game of Hope: On reaching this Key, one receives 2 marks.

Waite:

Contemporary: Opening, (or Closing), Access, Discovery, Revealing.

Functional: Change (of state).

What You Say: The Key reveals secrets.

34. Fish (The Fishes)

if near the Person, point to the acquisition of large fortune by marine enterprises and to a series of successful undertakings; if distant, they indicate the failure of any speculation, no matter how well projected or planned.

Dream Symbolism: Spiritual life. Communion. Being with others. Swimming deep.

Coffee Cards: THEY imply lucky events by water, if in the clear, which will either happen to the consulter or or improve the state of his affairs beyond the water. If they are in the thick, the consulter will fish in troubled water, and rely upon that which others have already lost before him. Surrounded with dots, they signify that his destiny calls to him some distant place.

Coffee Card Verse: Don't let yourself be caught with baits like the fish; circumspection is very necessary especially on a long journey.

Game of Hope: Reaching the Fish, one has to pay 2 marks.

Waite: Good News from Abroad, Invitation to Dinner.

Contemporary: Resources, Business, Money, Market, Potential.

Functional: Opportunity.

What You Say: The Fish bring resources.

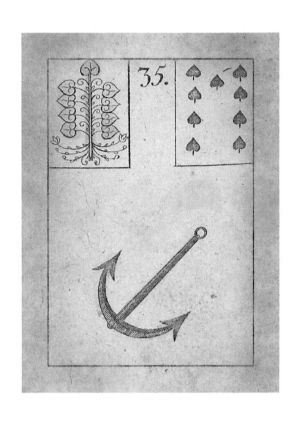

35. The Anchor

is a sign of successful enterprise at sea, of great advantage in trade, and of true love; but distant, it means a thorough disappointment in ideas, and inconstancy in love.

Dream Symbolism: Faith. Hope. Salvation. Safe Harbour. That to which we give faith.

Coffee Cards: The emblem of hope and commerce, implies successful benefits carried on by water and by land.

Land, if on the bottom of the cup; at the top and in the clear part, it shews constant love and unshaken fidelity. In the thick and clouded part it also denotes love, but tinctured with the inconsistency of the butterfly.

Coffee Card Verse: A person as honest as you in his dealings, will never want a rich harvest of gain; your wishes too are likely to be accomplished.

Game of Hope: This is the most important sheet of the whole game, insofar as the one, who comes to stay on this picture of Hope, has won the game and draws the whole cash-box or deposit.

Waite: Success in Business. Love and Fidelity. Inconsistency.

Contemporary: Hope, Long Time, Standstill, Stability.

Functional: Fixing.

What You Say: The Anchor is secure.

36. The Cross

is always a bad sign; if very near the person, you may hope that the misfortune will not last long.

Dream Symbolism: Burden. Being a martyr to some cause or memory. Carrying one's own cross. Self-suffering through attachment to something.

Coffee Cards: Be it one or more, it generally predicts adversities. It position varies, and so do the circumstances. If it be at the top, and in the clear, it shews that the misfortunes of the party will soon be at an end, or that he will easily get over them, but if it appears in the middle or at the end bottom in the thick party must expect many severe trials; if it appear with dots, either in the clear or the thick, it promises a speedy change of one's sorrow.

Coffee Card Verse: There is no misfortune however severe, that does not produce some good; hope therefore all will be for the best.

Game of Hope: So near to the luckiest field, the player is cheated as against his will he has to advance one step too far to the figure of the Cross, where he has to remain until another player takes this burden off him or he throws a double.

Waite: Death

Contemporary: Suffering, Burdens, Problems, Trouble.

Functional: Anxiety.

What You Say: The Cross is suffering.

Day 4. THREE CARD READING

Today we extend a three-card reading with everything we have learnt and give examples from real-life readings to further illustrate the method.

Hopefully, our previous three days have given us the basic practice to read three cards. We will now add a few important skills that come from experience – skills to help you refine and deliver the reading.

Firstly, we consider that we are going to conduct a reading by working through the cards from "right to left". We do not need to get confused about this, it simply – for now – means that the cards on the right influence the cards on the left, slightly shading or lightening its significance.

So, if we had CHILD + WHIP + COFFIN, the ending of the Coffin is to arguments of the Whip with regard to the Child – so actually, depending on the question, a very **positive** reading. This is my preferred way of reading, and I would call it "right to left" even if I look at the cards initially from left to right.

The confusion is just the way some people describe it, because we could get the same thing by reading "left to right" just by changing our language; "with regard to the child, there are arguments that will end".

Or we could read again, "left to right" but like this; "the child will be punished and become ill". These are all obviously either the same or very different readings.

It is only important that you decide how **you** will read it and then stick to that for a while before changing how you approach a reading. The cards will know – and will even help you! It also helps if you have a very specific question and read the cards as literally as possible.

If we conduct a three-card reading and receive the cards; BOOK + SCYTHE + HOUSE, and look up the "what you say" meanings we get, reading right to left:

The House is security

The Scythe means cutting

The Book brings knowledge

So, how might we piece those together and make a better reading, say, for the question, "How should I go about my family issue?"

Firstly, we always fix the question as our template by saying it out loud without pause or hesitation. We are answering the question, in Lenormand, by reading the cards. So, we say the question.

"You should go about your family issue by ..."

THEN we start to read the cards. This avoids us getting confused by card meanings and then trying to work them back to a question. It may seem easier to read the cards first, then apply them to the question, but experience is that it is way better to hold the question and slot the cards into it one at a time. Even if we go back and revise our card meaning as we read through them, at least we will be still doing this within the question.

So, "You should go about your family issue by ..." and then we take the first sentence and slot it in, changing the grammar slightly, "securing your house" ...

We might then consider whether the next card is better stated by joining it with an "and" or "so" or "because", but we can be free to try what works ...

"securing your house because it is time to cut" or

"securing your house so that a cut ..." or

"securing your house and a cutting will come".

That last version in our heads seems to slot into place, so we continue ...

"a cutting will come and bring knowledge".

Running that together, we can now smooth it out and play it forwards and backwards to refine it...

"You are advised to go about your family issue by first ensuring that your house is a place of security for everyone. This will cause a severing of ties with ~~something~~ someone that is (we get intuitive here) an unwanted influence in the home (then we go back and change "something" to "someone") and it will become open what they were up to".

Hopefully it will be obvious how the client should go about making their home a secure space for the family to discuss things, leading to a timely cutting and new information about the situation.

In effect 'security cutting knowledge'.

Book + Scythe + House

Exercise 1: Developing your Three-Card Reading

Now you try - with another three-card reading, putting it together, going backwards and forwards, running it through until you craft a neat delivery.

You must not expect to get it right first time, every time. The Lenormand is simple but it requires several passes sometimes, to see the simplicity. Just like life.

Example Three-Card Readings

Here are a few examples from my own client readings which may serve to illustrate real readings. I have abbreviated these to demonstrate the key points.

Three Card Reading 1

Q. How can I gain more recognition in my workplace?

MOON + FISH + GARDEN

Recognition + Resources + Meetings

Whilst this may appear a convenient set of cards chosen to illustrate a question, it is an actual reading which was selected to show the direct nature of the Lenormand cards.

The MOON finds itself next to the FISH. This speaks of good fortune and a life purpose that will bring recognition. The *Phillippe Sheet* writes that the MOON "is a sign of great honours, fortune and fame" and next to the FISH it is likely to bring additional "large fortune ... and successful undertakings".

The FISH next to the GARDEN foretells that success will come from networking; to visit "very respectable company". Success, then, will come from reaching out to other people directly and offering them your resources, which will reflect well upon oneself.

This is a very literal answer and almost states the obvious. However, sometimes the obvious is obvious for a reason.

Three Card Reading 2

Will the fortune of my family be happy?

Bouquet (9) + House (4) + Ring (25)

In this three-card reading asking about the welfare of the family there is a gift (BOUQUET) through a house (HOUSE) contract/marriage (RING). Reading "right to left", there is an agreement that must be entered into about the home affairs to bring about attention and a gift.

This is a very favourable reading but also suggests that the RING in a form of a contract should be checked to ensure that all is in writing and tightly bound up.

Three Card Reading 3

Q. What will happen regarding the financial impact of the accident?

BEAR (15) + LETTER (27) + STORK (17)

This reads as a fair and pragmatic communication returning from the accident. There will be an equal return (STORK, payment, given the question is 'financial') requested by writing (LETTER) in a BEAR-ish fashion. So, the client will not be let off the hook nor will they be treated unfairly, or advantage be taken.

It also seems that it will be a fair price given and the woman involved in the accident has a maternal authority with whom it will be easy to deal. It is a case where there is no need to draw other cards as it is self-explanatory. There are no bad cards in the reading, so there is no need to express further concern or divine more deeply.

Three Card Reading 4 (Alternative Method)

Q. What can I do to improve my health following birth?

In this case, I chose to use an alternative method, where I decide on a 'significator' or 'key-card' and then look for where it appears in a shuffled deck. I then read the two cards either side of it.

The first step is to shuffle the deck and focus on the card related to health, in the Lenormand this is the TREE. I then go through the cards and locate the TREE card and look at the cards either side of the TREE:

BOOK (26) +TREE (5) +RING (25)

The answer is that the client must commit to learning more about their own health. There is also an indication with BOOK (knowledge) and TREE (health) that it is a question of improving mental health as well as learning more about healthy living. Whilst I do not give medical advice I discuss with the client – which they have already considered – that they seek an additional therapeutic approach to their health.

The RING can be considered as a contemporary symbol of a "holistic" approach. We must remember that the original interpretations written for the cards are now historic; the BIRDS may have meant 'chatter' a few hundred years ago, but now they are more likely to mean 'Twitter'.

Three Card Reading 5 (Alternative Method)

Q. Will the Sitter retire from work at the end of the year?

Using the alternative method of locating a specific key-card in a shuffled deck, I look for the card that corresponds to endings. In the Lenormand this can either be the SCYTHE or the COFFIN, and in this instance, I use the COFFIN, as it is a **permanent** ending from work. I look for that card and locate the two cards either side of it:

FOX (14) + COFFIN (8) + LETTER (27)

This is plainly "A Letter communicates Ending of Work".

The Sitter then wants to know if there will be a golden handshake, in the form of severance pay?

We can elaborate further on this 3-card reading by keeping the cards in their positions and check through the deck for the card that corresponds to Money in the Lenormand. The card that corresponds to money is the FISHES. I then look at the cards either side of the FISHES:

SHIP (3) +FISHES (34) + STAR (16)

The STAR bodes well, for it signifies "Good luck in all enterprises" according to the *Phillippe Sheet*. For fortune and money (FISHES) the SHIP brings the fortune to the Sitter "after a series of successful undertakings".

The sitter has been through a series of negotiations with her employers. This reading suggests that this will be effective, and she will benefit financially. However, there is a warning that any financial reward must be invested carefully and with as little risk as possible. The money must not be blown on a Caribbean cruise. I read this in this way because the historical context of the Ship carries the significance of foreign ventures which were always at risk to the investment.

A Deeper Reading

In this final example, I would like to show in brief that the Lenormand be used for deeper readings.

Q. How best to promote a better relationship with an estranged or distant relative?

TREE (5) + MAN (28) + KEY (33)

This indicates health and family roots (tradition) with a man in the centre and an unlocking or locking. We might read this simply as "roots of the man are the key" or "unlocking the man and his roots". This offers a very psychological interpretation. The man must be made sure of his own family traditions and roots.

Optional Exercise

Use the method of selecting and locating a 'key-card' with a real question, producing a three-card reading where the central card is the 'key-card' suitable for the question.

This is great practice towards the Grand Tableaux reading at the end of the week.

Day 5. NINE CARD READING (Rows)

Today, we simply repeat what we have learnt with three-card readings to conduct a nine-card reading. Tomorrow, I give several real examples in addition to one today, but you can read ahead a little if it is helpful.

To conduct a nine-card reading, we simply shuffle and lay out **three rows of three cards**, making a square of nine.

Make sure you ask a clear question!

We then read the top row as things 'bearing down' on the situation, past, present and future. The middle row is simply past, present and future. The bottom row are things that we can change or influence – so, "advice", past, present and future.

The bottom-left card is 'advice in the past', then, and this tends to be how you can see something better in the past, let it go, or resolve a past part of the present situation.

I will first give a real example, then I will present todays exercise – which is to conduct a nine-card reading.

A Nine Card Reading of Three Rows

Q. What is the best prospect for improving my finances?

CLOUDS + STAR + SCYTHE

BIRDS + COFFIN + BOOK

SUN + BOUQUET + DOG

On the top row, bearing down on the client, we have the SCYTHE in the future, which is a card of danger – and an issue of timing. This affects the STAR which is in the present position, indicating that happiness is under pressure from time. The CLOUDS are the uncertainty from the past. There is no clear indication of stability in the past from which to build in the present. In fact, as per the Philippe Sheet; *"but if near clouds, it means a long series of unhappy accidents"*.

This shows us (correctly, as it is confirmed by the client) that there have been several incidents in the past which have significantly affected their finances out of the blue; there has been no chance to build up a stable income, despite following a vision; and that there is a timing issue to make a particular payment which is now bearing down on the client.

A 9 Card Layout

Interestingly, we have no specific work or financial cards in the row, such as the Fish, Fox, Bear, Ship or Tower. This suggests that it is a personal or emotional issue rather than a purely practical constraint in finances.

In the centre row, the BOOK finds itself next to the COFFIN and tells of discovering a secret or a revelation which brings about an ending. The COFFIN is next to the BIRDS which indicates the ending of hardships. A revelation and new openness will win the situation over. If we word it another way, the current situation will end, bringing about a new opening in the future. The BIRDS in the past show that previous distractions - or the opinion and advice of other people - are no longer relevant.

In the bottom row of advice, the DOG finds itself sat next to the BOUQUET. A faithful and sincere friend brings the gift of "much happiness in every respect". The BOUQUET is next to the SUN and "points to happiness and pleasure, as it its beams spread warmth and light" in the situation in question.

There is clearly a transition point in the financial life of the client currently, and the cards suggest that past performance is causing them to doubt their future. Whilst this seems obvious in any case, it is clear confirmation that the cards have picked up the situation.

In the past, they have been distracted by the advice or chatter of other people, and now they must write a new narrative for themselves in the future – a new book.

They are advised to trust someone whose gift will bring them much happiness and support – and this in turn will improve their finances.

Exercise 1

Conduct your own nine-card reading with a real question. Read the central row first, then the upper row followed by the bottom row for advice.

If you get stuck, write down the keywords or "what you say" sentences and use the first exercises to build up your reading in smaller sections.

You can also walk away from the reading for a little while and then return to it with a new perspective – sometimes a Lenormand reading can first appear meaningless and then suddenly become blindingly obvious.

Day 6. NINE CARD READING (Columns)

We will first look at another real reading, and this time introduce the reading of the three vertical columns. This adds even more depth to the reading and prepares us for the Grand Tableaux.

A Nine Card Reading with Columns

Q: How can I gain balance again in my emotional state?

In this optional method, I choose a 'key card' (not always *the* Key card!) or 'significator' to place in the centre of the reading first, and then I lay out eight cards around it in a square. This is an alternative method which you can also try!

I choose the HEART card for the central key-card in this case, as it is clearly a question about emotions.

As we have already seen, the top cards bear down on the situation whilst the bottom cards can be affected by the Client. On the middle row, the card to the left simply represents the past and the card to the right represents the future.

RIDER (1) + FOX (14) + BOOK (26)

MOUNTAIN (21) + HEART (24) + GARDEN (20)

SUN (31) + BOUQUET (9) + DOG (18)

In this reading, I read the direct past and future cards in the middle line first, as they are behind and ahead of the key-card. This is identical to the way we read cards in the Grand Tableaux - so is perfect practice.

The MOUNTAIN card shows that there have been obstacles and challenges in the past, so the Sitter had to find an alternative way around their situation. Their emotional life took some sort of detour from its expected route and destination. The GARDEN card in the future shows that this detour will actually put them in a more open relationship with other people. It is a case of not climbing the mountain by oneself but enjoying the garden of life in good company.

The cards pressing down upon the Sitter show that in the past, the situation was changed by something unexpected and new – a delivery of news which caused the detour below it [RIDER above the MOUNTAIN]. We can read the cards above and below each other in this little square, as again this is practice for the Grand Tableaux. We will return to this column when we look at the bottom line.

The future pressing issue is the BOOK. This means that the client must learn something new, and (or) remain an open book. It is about – in context of the original question – remaining open emotionally, expressing oneself and not keeping secrets. We can check this when we see that the BOOK is above the GARDEN. The Sitter must become open in a social sense, widening their ability to learn from other people as well as sharing their own self with a wider circle.

The FOX in the present shows that the issue bearing down upon the Sitter is their own sense of self-sufficiency. They may feel as if they are being out-foxed, or indeed, need to become foxier. This indicates a sense of self-worth which is weighing on their mind and heart. As this is somewhat negative, as I was doing the reading, I pointed out to the Sitter that the answer was below in that column.

This is the BOUQUET card. Their self-worth is a gift to themselves, and to others. There is something which will come out of this situation which will be a great gift to the Sitter and to those who are in their heart.

We now look at the bottom row for the possibilities for action, in terms of dealing with the past and setting up the best for the future, in the context of the question. We can also now complete any column which we may have already started to read in the first two rows.

The SUN is in the past, and this shows that the good luck and expansion that the Sitter enjoyed in the past is now something on which they must continue to draw.

There is a lot of energy already in the last which is not separate to the present. We can see too that this is the key to the RIDER and the MOUNTAIN situation in the past – even though there was news that caused a diversion, there was great success throughout the past. So, there is still much light to see the way ahead, and the MOUNTAIN is now in the past. The way ahead is clear, even with the change in journey; it was a detour that can still cast a great light on the present and future situation, as well as the emotional state of the Sitter.

The DOG is in the future of the affection row, indicating that the Sitter can be a loyal friend – to their own emotional state. They can trust the DOG even though they also have to reconcile themselves to the FOX. In fact, these two cards are the key to their reconciliation; one is domestic, one is wild. These two parts of themselves seek reconciliation; the loyal friend and the self-sufficient partner.

The DOG is the final key, in the bottom-right corner, under the BOOK and GARDEN. An increasing sense of openness, expression to others and authenticity to self is the answer to reconcile the current emotional state.

Exercise 1

Consider the following nine-card reading and how you would interpret it for this question from a small business "How can we gain more income for project X?"

The nine cards drawn are:

MOUNTAIN (21) + ANCHOR (25) + DOG (18)

BOOK (26) + FISHES (34) + TREE (5)

SUN (31) + BOUQUET (9) + GENTLEMAN (28)

What does the centre line say, and what is bearing down on the project? Will it generally be easy or difficult to gain more income for the project? What does the business have most control over, and how might they proceed?

Exercise 2

Conduct a nine-card reading using both the rows and columns for your own chosen question.

Day 7. THE GRAND TABLEAUX

On this final day, we now turn to the Grand Tableaux reading using all 36 cards – bringing together everything we have learnt this week.

A Grand Tableaux is a layout of all 36 cards in four rows of nine cards – alternatively, four rows of eight cards with four cards placed the bottom of the layout. We will stick to four rows of nine.

There are many techniques that can be employed in reading this layout, including Houses, Chaining, Distance, Facing, and Knighting. In this book, I will just be covering Houses and Chaining – but you do not even need these to conduct a good reading.

CHAINING

To conduct a Grant Tableaux (big picture) reading we can use all the skills we have learnt this week. We can start by using the simplest way of reading two cards – like we learnt with the DOG and the HOUSE seven days ago – and just repeat it across the whole spread.

We usually look to the GENTLEMAN or LADY card, depending on the Sitter, and read from that card.

In fact, it is good to lay out a Grand Tableaux (GT) reading even if you only read a few pairs in it, because it will get you used to seeing a lay out of all the cards. Sometimes, even as an absolute beginner, you will see a particular pattern that has profound significance to the question.

Of course, we want to do a lot more with the Grand Tableaux, and there are many additional layers in reading this spread – but for now, we will just add one method, which is CHAINING.

Chaining is a method of linking cards and their positions ("houses") throughout a Grand Tableaux. It allows us to easily weave a story and it also deepens the whole reading – sometimes to very accurate and profound significance.

You can read the GT today *without* chaining (and houses), but I offer it here, so you can have a go at it if you want!

First, we just have to know about the "houses", and this is why we spent our second day learning about the order and numbering of the cards. As you continue to practice, this will become easier – for today, we will just do the method step-by-step and give a full example of using it.

HOUSES

When we lay out a Grand Tableaux, we lay out the cards in one of two ways. In this case we are using a simple rectangle of **4 rows by 9 columns**. So, we lay nine cards across in a line, then another nine cards below them, until we have four rows of cards below each other in a rectangle.

Now, there are no real "positional meanings" to the cards in a Grand Tableaux as there might be in a tarot card spread, such as the middle card being "Your Situation Now", or a top-right card being "Hopes and Fears".

But – there are "Houses". The Houses are actually very straight-forward. Imagine that we have already laid out the deck in numbered order in the same pattern. So, we have the Rider (1) laid down first, then the Clover (2), then the Ship (3) and so on. The Cross (36) would be in the final position at the bottom right of the rectangle.

This would be one of the ways in which the cards of the *Game of Hope* would be laid out for a parlour game.

This gives us "meanings" for those positions, and it also gives us a connection to another card through chaining.

The Houses

We aren't covering the meanings, but you can find out more about those in the recommended books at the end of this book. They are pretty straight-forward, and based on the card, so the first position of the Rider (1) is considered "News" in the situation. The final position of the Cross (36) is either the outcome or the biggest challenge of the situation.

So, if we had the Fish in the first position and the Scythe in the final position, it might suggest "News about Resources" and a "Challenge about Time". If the question was "Will I get a promotion in this current job", this reading might indicate something quite negative!

In chaining, we start with one card – any card that we are reading in the Tableaux, say the Lady card for a woman, and look at the position it is in, and see the card which would be in that position in sequence. This is the "house" (not to be confused with the card called the House!) and we can then go look for that card in the reading and read it as part of a story.

In turn, we then see which position and house that card is in and go look for that card – and so on, weaving a story, until we return to a card we have read already and end the story.

Make sense? It's easier to do than explain – and you can even have a client do it with you, particularly if you get a sheet on which the houses/positions are already marked. Another trick is to simply lay out another Lenormand deck on the table first, in sequence, and lay your reading cards on top of those cards.

Example of Chaining

Here is an example which was taken from a real reading. You can look at each card to get a feeling of how I put the card and house together. These are also from a chain, so you can follow along with the chain as we put the meaning together:

The CHILD is in the house of the ROD; there is a situation of Quarrels. The inner child of the Sitter may feel like a child that is being chastised as she is in the house of conflict.

The ROD is in the house of the MOON, "the sign of great honours and fortune", this means well for the querents issue but currently affects her self-worth.

The MOON is the house of the WAY. What is reflected on the Sitter is coming from the choices they are making.

The WAY is in the house of the RING a commitment to the way. These choices are about commitment.

The RING is the house of the GARDEN this is a meeting of "respectable company" but means that the Sitter is trying to commit to too much or too many people.

The GARDEN is the house of the BEAR, the over-commitment is an issue arising from the Mother of the Sitter and her upbringing.

The BEAR is the house of the STORK, "A change of abode" away from the mother is advised, and the STORK is the house of the FOX, becoming self-sufficient.

As the Client presently lives with her mother, this reading has immediate impact.

Exercise 1. The Grand Tableaux Layout.

Shuffle all the cards and lay them out face-up in four rows of nine cards.

A. Locate the GENTLEMAN card if you are male or the LADY card if you are female.

Conduct a nine-card reading around that card.

If it is close to the edge of the layout, read the cards that are close to the LADY or GENTLEMAN. If there is nothing to their right, the answer is in the past, if there is nothing to their left, the past can be ignored. If there is nothing above them, they have a lot of choice, if there is nothing below them, they have a lot pressing down on them.

B. Next, choose an area in life, such as relationships, locate the appropriate card in the layout, the HEART, and conduct a nine-card reading around that card.

Optionally, select another area, such as work; and read around the FOX, BEAR or ANCHOR as seems appropriate.

If you are asking about relationship, look at the distance and positions of the LADY and GENTLEMAN, and the cards between them.

C. Conduct a chain from the LADY or GENTLEMAN card, using the houses. You can also chain from any other card, such as the FISH for finances, etc.

Example of a Grand Tableaux

I now give a real example of a difficult work situation which required specific advice – and show how the Lenormand clearly gave advice which the client followed – successfully.

This reading was conducted as a detailed follow-up to the client who had asked about early retirement. They wanted more advice about how they responded to the situation, so I conducted a GT – this time using the 4 x 8 + 4 variation.

Q. Should I take retirement or fight over the overpayment that is being taken back from me by my work?

The FOX (Work) sits next to the LADY. It is a pressing matter.

The LADY is looking for new direction as she faces the past card of the STAR (navigation/direction) and this sits next to the WAYS of Choice.

I then look at the WAYS card and see it is in the house of the RING - she needs to be committed to her choice, with no half-hearted measures.

As I like to make sure I tell the sitter a little bit about their future at the beginning of the reading, I look to the cards to the right of their personal card, i.e. the LADY.

Ahead of the LADY is the FOX + SUN + TOWER + SCYTHE + WHIP.

A Grand Tableaux (4 x 8 + 4 layout)

I read these as a line and say that there will be good luck (SUN), as this "lying near, points to happiness and pleasure, as it beams spread light and warmth".

The TOWER is very clear as it shows an institution - a school – which is the Sitters place of work. I apply the cards to the right and this shows that she will need to cut away (SCYTHE) from the school and end the strife and conflict (WHIP).

I now turn to look at the main card for the situation, which I chose to be the FOX. This is also because the Sitter is in a situation where their own personal ability is being challenged. I need to know how the FOX will deal with cutting away from the TOWER.

The FOX is in the house of the GENTLEMAN.

This tells me – and is immediately confirmed by the Sitter – that the whole issue of her own ability relates to her partner. There is some issue between them, likely an issue of power in the relationship. The FOX does not probably like being in the house of the GENTLEMAN.

I now link the GENTLEMAN in a chain of Houses to explore that situation in more depth. This can sometimes (as it will in this reading) be a long chain, particularly when several issues are all bound up together. In some readings, a chain will come to an end very quickly, usually meaning that the response is obvious and just needs some actual action.

I see that the GENTLEMAN card is in the house of the SNAKE.

I recognise this as a gentleman who seeks to undermine the Sitters own will. The Serpent is a traditional symbol of temptation and devious devices. In Lenormand, it is a hidden threat, sometimes right under your feet.

We can find out more about this danger by following the chain of links through the houses and cards.

The SERPENT is the house of the KEY.

I interpret the KEY as "success coming from a wish or a plan". The fact that the KEY is in the House of the SNAKE signifies that the Sitter must unlock the situation themselves to avoid being bitten by the snake.

The theme of self-determination is being repeated in several of these links, as it often is in a Lenormand reading.

To see what action will unlock the situation and avoid the snake, I follow the chain of the KEY card.

The KEY is the house of the FISHES.

According to the *Phillipe Sheet*, the FISHES represents "the acquisition of large fortune and series of successful undertakings".

So, it seems as if the Sitter needs to use and somehow hold on to money (or their other resource, time) as the most important factor in unlocking their position and avoiding danger.

The Sitter again understands what this means, as they explain they have been given money (by the TOWER) but also asked to return it. They would usually have done so, but the reading is suggesting that it is important to hold their position and not be undercut by any Snakes.

Looking to see how the sitter can protect her resources we look to see where the FISHES card is placed. The FISHES card is the house of the CHILD, this is interesting because the sitter works with children and the cards are telling her that she has done well from this work.

The FISHES being in the house of the CHILD can also be read as suggesting that the sitter must be true to her own authentic truth. She has always acted in good faith and with pure intent. The resources the FISHES will materialise if she sticks to her true feelings.

"The person moves in good society and is full of kindness towards everybody", and the Sitter should be true to this.

Because of this reading, the Sitter chose to ignore her partners advice, stick to her guns, and the School backed down from their repayment demands, actually releasing her with a good settlement.

There were also several self-empowerment and other issues that emerged from this reading which were of relevance and use to the Sitter.

Well done! You can now approach a GT reading with Lenormand in just seven days, even if there's a lifetime of practice and discovery ahead of you in the cards! I recommend the book *Learning Lenormand* (Goodwin & Katz) for your next step into intermediate and advanced methods, and the full history of the deck.

I will now finish by giving ten tips for your future experience and wish you a grand adventure with this wonderful deck!

Ten More Ways to Learn Lenormand

1. Read Books.

The more the better, and the more in different languages that you can, the better. Many readers across Europe learnt from books, or books have written down what other readers have used in their readings.

In writing "Learning Lenormand", Tali Goodwin spent two years purchasing and reading French, German, Portuguese and Brazilian books. Although it can be initially complex, dealing with ambiguities of language and contradictions (sometimes within the same book, never mind between different authors), it soon pays off – your readings will be deeper, more flexible and fluent as you create your own accent of the literal Lenormand language.

2. Study the History.

The Lenormand has developed over a shorter period of time, and in a more constrained way, than Tarot, for example, until recently. It makes it far easier to trace the development of the lexicon and grammar of the card meanings, starting with the Game of Hope. We can then range through cartomantic meanings and associations, and symbolic systems such as dream interpretation and coffee-grind readings, etc. This will again widen your ability to appreciate the symbols and create readings.

3. Practice.

There are many online venues, such as the LEARNING LENORMAND study group on Facebook, where you can practice with others.

4. Compare Notes.

Read what experienced readers have to say on their craft. Whether they learnt from their "grandmother" or picked it up over four decades of reading from their home, making it up from what worked, everyone has an opportunity to share their methods and styles.

5. Stick to a Deck or Two.

To start, don't get too carried away with deck-purchasing unless you are a collector or enthusiast for different decks. Whilst we promote the innovative and beautiful new decks now appearing on a weekly basis, for a beginner, we recommend the Piatnik, Dondorf, Blue Owl, the Original Lenormand (from the original 1800 game of Hope by J. K. Hechtel), or whichever deck appeals most to you. Once you have got reasonably confident in one deck out of maybe three or four you have purchased, then dive into the cartomantic ocean waiting for you with many possible new decks!

6. Take Courses.

As with any subject, you will learn differently with different teachers, no matter what the content. It is important you find someone who teaches in a way that works for you. There's nothing more frustrating than good content presented badly, or in a confusing manner. If you are paying for a course, then check whether you are getting value compared to "free" content online. A paid course should be so because it features an experienced teacher in the subject, high quality research or material, or high production values – or a combination of those things, which cost money to produce.

7. Ignore Talking about Tradition.

Ignore anything you might read about "tradition". Stating that there is a definitive singular tradition (whether based on language, geography or teacher) is a very difficult thing to prove. There is a lot of ongoing research into this, and until it is published, there will be a lot of "noise" about "THE German tradition" or "THE French tradition". It would be fantastic if we could get ten different (and isolated from each other) readers in Germany, speaking German only, each of whom we could demonstrate learnt from several generations back. We could then interview them, and their parents and grandparents.

We could then compare their *lexicon* (card meanings, i.e. FISH = MONEY), and *grammar* (card combinations, i.e. FISH + CLOVER = Luck in Money). We could then check that all 36 meanings and any combinations were IDENTICAL across all ten readers, and their parents and grandparents. We could then ensure that they were NOT identical to anything published or had consistent variations. THEN we could begin to suspect an entirely separate oral tradition, belonging to a particular language or geography – and we could then look to trace any written source, such as cartomantic manuals in old German dating back to the last several centuries. A big job ...

8. Stick to One Approach.

Stick to one set of "rules" or meanings. Read left to right, or right to left, read the Bear as Money, a job or mothers, but only one of those things (meaning you'll need another card for the other things), and so on. But stick to one set. Read, practice, and over time you'll calibrate that to your experience.

As an example, one reader (in tarot) always read the 5 of Pentacles as "poverty", but consistently got financially comfortable people for whom that card was coming up. He started to ask them about their situations, and soon discovered that the card was more about "deferred comfort", that's to say, people investing for the long-term, going on an expensive course so they couldn't enjoy the comforts of life, etc., planning for the long-term. So now, for him, that card means that, rather than "poverty" as he started using. Just test one set of meanings until it snaps into place.

9. Read More Cards than One at a Time.

Use as many cards as you can. In Lenormand, I feel, I learnt best by starting with the Grand Tableau, even though I only read a few cards in it to begin with. I then branched out, rather than got frustrated with trying to make sense out of two or three cards. It was avoiding what I see often with beginners, "Oh, I am doing two cards for my daily draw, and I got "CLOVER + FISH", lucky money, or money bringing luck, any other ideas?" Well, that's it, really! I'd be more interested then to know where that was coming from, how I could recognise – or indeed – encourage this situation. And I'd need more cards to tell me; where's the Fox, the Bear – is it an opportunity at work? Where's the Mountain, the Snake, the Cross – anything to stop it happening? And so on. At least with starting with the Grand Tableau you have the opportunity to read outwards as and when you can, and with context.

10. Have Fun.

Have fun, explore, take your time, and bring your own voice to the cards. We feel the Lenormand has a unique "literal Lenormand" language in the world of cartomancy. It will be a while before the current interest settles into longer-term usage in a wider audience. Some things will re-surface and be taken up by a lot of people, other things will remain peculiar to just one reader. There are still new discoveries and insights to be made, and this will take time. Don't waste it by doing anything other than enjoying your own personal studying and reading of the cards.

Conclusion

In this book I've shared the first essential steps to get you reading your Lenormand cards with confidence. It will take practice, but if you are kind to yourself and keep going, it will be easy to soon have these cards as your personal friend!

I hope you have found this book to be informative and thank you for taking the time to purchase and read it.

My key aim to share genuine, fresh cartomantic teaching techniques that leave you wanting to learn more. If you have liked what you have read and would like to learn more about fortune-telling please do come along and join me and many thousands of other readers in the www.tarotassociation.net website where you will discover a wealth of friendly, innovative and lively fun with the cards.

Wishing you a full and happy life journey.

With love Andrea x

Kindle Tarot Books & Series

Check out all these other books and series for original and exciting ways in which you can use a deck of tarot cards to change your life.

Gated Spreads Series

Set 1

Book 1: The Tarot Shaman (Contact Your Animal Spirit)

Book 2: Gates of Valentine (Love & Relationships)

Book 3: The Resurrection Engine (Change Your Life)

Set 2

Book 4: Palace of the Phoenix (Alchemy)

Book 5: Garden of Creation (Creativity & Inspiration)

Book 6: Ghost Train (Explore Your Past)

Set 3

Tarot Temple

Book 1: Create a Tarot Dream Temple

Book 2: The Sacred Altar

Book 3: Tarot Temple Tools

Book 4: Banishing Negativity & Unbalanced Forces

Book 5: Purification of your Temple & Life

Book 6: Consecration of your Temple & Life

Book 7: Divining with the Gods

Tarosophy KickStart Series

Volume I.

Book I: Tarot Flip - Reading Tarot Straight from the Box

Book II: Tarot Twist – 78 New Spreads and Methods [paperback]

Book III: Tarot Inspire – Tarot for a Spiritual Life

Tarot Life Series

Tarot Life: A revolutionary method to change your life in 12 Kindle booklets. Also includes membership of a private discussion group on Facebook to share and explore your experiences with over a thousand other readers.

1. Discover Your Destiny

2. Remove The Blocks

3. Make Decisions Better

4. Enter the Flow

5. Ride the Lion

6. Connect to Service

7. Find Equality

8. Die To Your Self

9. Entering Unity

10. Becoming the Real

Also in Print and Kindle

Tarosophy: A ground-breaking book packed with original ideas. The book also includes 50 unique exercises for Tarot and an extended method of using the Inner Guide Meditation as given here.

Around the Tarot in 78 Days: The ideal beginner book, a three-month course through every card. An award-winning book, recognized by the COVR New Age Industry Award for Best Divination Book 2013.

Tarot Face to Face: Take your tarot out of the box and into life!

Secrets of the Waite-Smith Tarot: Learn the real meanings of the world's most popular tarot deck [Spring 2015, pub. Llewellyn Worldwide].

Tarot Turn Vol. 1 - 3: A massive crowd-sourced reference guide to all 12,200 possible combinations of reversed Tarot card pairs.

Websites & Resources

If you enjoy new learning and want many more ways to use your Tarot deck, we encourage you to explore our websites. You are also welcome to join us in the Tarosophy Tarot Association, where as a member you will instantly receive thousands of pages of materials, and tarot video courses for every level.

We look forward to seeing you soon on your Tarot journey!

Tarosophy Tarot Associations

http://www.tarotassociation.net

Tarot Professionals Facebook Group

http://www.facebook.com/groups/tarotprofessionals

Free Tarot Card Meanings & Spreads

http://www.mytarotcardmeanings.com

Notes

[1] See Goodwin, T. & Katz, M. *The English Lenormand* (Keswick: Forge Press, 2013).

[2] Translation by Steph Engert, http://www.starlight-dragon-tarotdeck.eu

[3] This section has a deeper significance for advanced readers. I have used variations of four ways of reading each card. These are the four levels; literal, symbolic, extended and secret. Readers of Tarosophy books will see these are Kabbalistic levels. To illustrate these four levels, I have used variations of "is" (literal), "means" (symbolic), "brings" (extended) and "reveals" (secret); so "The Tree **is** health" is a literal reading, whereas we could also say "The Tree **brings** stability" which is an extended reading. Advanced readers might find insight and inspiration when experimenting with these four little words for the levels.

Printed in Great Britain
by Amazon